Little Ant and the Mantis

S.M.R. Saia

Illustrations by Tina Perko

Little Ant was in a bad mood. First, he tried to lift a crumb that was too heavy for him. It knocked him off balance, fell off his back, and rolled down the anthill. "I don't like crumbs!" Little Ant said.

Next, Little Ant had to wait in line for his breakfast. There were many ants in front of him, and they were all moving very slowly. Little Ant was very hungry. "I don't like lines!" Little Ant complained.

Later, Buddy Ant would not stop giving him advice. "That crumb is too small, Little Ant," Buddy Ant said first. "That crumb is too big, Little Ant," Buddy Ant said next. "Why haven't you picked up any crumbs?" Buddy Ant demanded a few minutes later.

Little Ant felt like he was going to explode. "I don't like advice," Little Ant said. "I don't like gathering crumbs, I don't like lines, and right now I don't like you, Buddy Ant!"

This hurt Buddy Ant's feelings. "I am sorry, Little Ant," Buddy Ant said as he walked away. "I was only trying to help."

Uncle Ant asked Little Ant what was wrong. "Nothing ever goes right for me!" Little Ant cried.

Uncle Ant smiled. "You must count your blessings, Little Ant," Uncle Ant said. "You have many good things in your life."

"I have a lot of bad things in my life," Little Ant declared.

"Think harder, Little Ant," Uncle Ant told him.

Little Ant walked off by himself and thought harder. He did not always get credit for all the things that he did for the colony. He was the smallest ant in the anthill, and sometimes his friends were too busy to play with him. And on top of all of that, he had to share everything! I am the unluckiest and most ill-treated ant in the whole world, he decided.

Suddenly, the ground beneath him began to shudder, and a great shadow loomed over him. A human! Little Ant was about to cry out when something scooped him up and dropped him down, down, down onto a pile of other stunned insects.

Little Ant tried to run, but he bounced off of something hard and landed back against the others. "Ow!" Little Ant cried. "What is that?" He got up and began to run again, and again he bounced off of an invisible wall. Then Little Ant felt himself rising up into the air, and a bumpy ride began. He rolled around with the other insects, feeling off-balance and sick to his stomach.

When the ride stopped, they were turned upside down. Little Ant and the others landed with a thud on a smooth, white floor.

"This is the worst day ever!" he thought to himself.

Little Ant was furious. He put his hand on the smooth, hard, invisible wall and began to walk. He walked around and around and around in a circle, but the invisible wall did not end.

A praying mantis stretched, took a deep breath, sat down with his legs crossed, and folded his hands in front of him. The third time that Little Ant passed him, the praying mantis said hello.

"How do I get out of here?" Little Ant cried.

"I don't know," the praying mantis answered.

Little Ant pointed to the other unhappy bugs. "What is this place?" he demanded. "Why are we here?"

"I don't know," the praying mantis said.

Little Ant did not like those answers. He did not like the other insects. He did not like the invisible wall. Little Ant walked as far away as he could from the praying mantis, which was not very far, and sat down to wait.

The day was long. Little Ant was bored, and hungry, and lonely. The other insects were worried and restless. But the praying mantis still sat with a peaceful smile on his face. That peaceful smile made Little Ant even angrier.

Little Ant marched over to the praying mantis and said, "We are prisoners here! Our lives are ruined and may be over! What do you have to be happy about?" The praying mantis opened his eyes and said, "There is always something to be happy about."

"There is not!" Little Ant insisted.

"Sit with me," the praying mantis said. "Sit quietly beside me, and see if your mind begins to change."

Still fuming, Little Ant sat down beside him. Many thoughts flew around inside of Little Ant's mind. He had angry thoughts and bored thoughts. He had hungry thoughts and lonely thoughts. Little Ant sat and thought for a very long time, until finally he wasn't thinking of anything. He was just sitting quietly, feeling his breath coming in and going out, and he felt better. Little Ant opened his eyes and stood up.

"Have you found something to be happy about?" the praying mantis asked.

"Yes," Little Ant said. "I am happy to be an ant. I am just as much of an ant here as I am back in the anthill, and ants solve problems by working together."

Little Ant introduced himself to the other insects and pointed through the invisible wall to where the smooth, white floor came to an end. "If we can push the invisible wall far enough," Little Ant said, "I think we can escape."

All of the insects pushed. Little by little, the invisible wall began to move. They pushed until there was a crack big enough for the largest insects to fit through. Then they took turns scrambling out. They were free!

"Thank you, Little Ant!" the insects called as they hurried back to the lives they had been taken from. Little Ant waved goodbye to them. Then he turned to the praying mantis and said, "Thank you."

"My pleasure, Little Ant," the praying mantis said. "Remember, there is always a reason to be happy."

Little Ant ran back to the anthill, where the first thing he did was throw his arms around Buddy Ant. "I am sorry, Buddy Ant! I do like crumbs, and it is not too hard to wait in line for my food, and I do like you," Little Ant said. "All of these things are my blessings, and I am so happy to have them!" Buddy Ant grinned widely. He was very proud to be someone's blessing.

Not far away, Uncle Ant smiled. He couldn't wait for Little Ant to tell the story of what had caused his change of heart.

Copyright 2018 by S.M.R. Saia
Illustrations by Tina Perko

Free activities for the Little Ant books are available at
http://littleantbooks.com.

Follow Little Ant on Facebook and Instagram at @littleantnews. Learn more about Little Ant's life; be the first to know when there are new Little Ant activities available for free download, and get cool news about insects you can share with your kids!

All rights reserved. No part of this book may be reproduced or used in any manner whatsoever without the express written permission of the publisher.

Published by Shelf Space Books
http://shelfspacebooks.com

ISBN: 978-1-945713-28-6

CPSIA information can be obtained
at www.ICGtesting.com
Printed in the USA
LVHW070032011019
632799LV00019B/105/P